CONSULTATIVE SELLING SKILLS

REVISED AND UPDATED

CLOSE MORE SALES, BUILD TRUST AND
IMPROVE CUSTOMER LOYALTY THROUGH
CONSULTATIVE SALES PROCESSES AND SKILLS

Dr. John N. Brennan

Copyright © 2014 Dr. John N. Brennan
All rights reserved.

ISBN: 1499174454
ISBN 13: 9781499174458

FORWARD

The purpose of this revised and updated book is to educate and inform sales reps, sales managers and VPs about the reasons you should take a second look at the way you approach selling in the new digital age. The book comes as a result of twenty-five years of coaching and training sales people to sell, while selling the moving target of my own company's services. If you believe that the business world is changing, that the way customers buy is changing, and that the profession of selling is changing, this is the book for you. You should read this book if you work inside a small, medium or large organization. Consultants, lawyers, accountants, health care professionals in private practice - you all sell your services. This book is also for you.

ABOUT THE AUTHOR

John Brennan, Ed.D

Dr. John Brennan has focused his career on sales training - designing and delivering sales training programs in North America, Asia, Europe, Australia, and the Middle East. His specific expertise includes sales management, sales assessments, sales skills enhancement, business development, sales coaching, and instructional design.

Dr. Brennan received his doctorate from the University of Rochester where his dissertation researched the effects of training on the development of empathy.

To help a European auto manufacturer launch its most successful new product in history, he designed and delivered a global sales training program. He recruited, trained and managed sales trainers to deliver the courses. Other clients have included Gannett Company, GlaxoSmithKline, Prudential, Click2Learn, and Volkswagen.

Dr. Brennan has developed the selling skills of hundreds of sales reps and managers in intense, small-group, interactive, classroom-style courses. As a trainer/facilitator, he has achieved outstanding participant satisfaction ratings.

He is also the publisher of Sales Coaching Matters, a monthly newsletter and is a member of the American Society for Training and Development.

TABLE OF CONTENTS

Forward 3

About the Author 5

Chapter 1:   The Evolution of Consultative Selling 9

Chapter 2:   What Customers Want 11

Chapter 3:   Prospecting for New Customers 17

Chapter 4:   Listening to Customer Needs 27

Chapter 5:   Converting Prospects to Customers 33

Chapter 6:   Reading Customer Buying Styles 41

Chapter 7:   Preparing and Presenting Proposals to Customers 53

Chapter 8:   Managing Customer Objections 65

Chapter 9:   Getting Agreements with Customers 73

Chapter 10:   Negotiating with Customers 77

Chapter 11:   Summary and Next Steps 87

CHAPTER 1:
THE EVOLUTION OF CONSULTATIVE SELLING

And for a salesman, there is no rock bottom to the life. He's a man way out there in the blue, riding on a smile and a shoeshine.
— Arthur Miller, Death of a Salesman.

While selling has been a central activity in our world, computers, global competition, the migration from the industrial age to the information age and now to the digital age, have changed the way customers buy. By the middle ages in Europe, the emerging merchant class had gathered some power for itself and established the first rules of the market. In this marketplace, the merchants who could sell and negotiate the best were the most successful. Soon the industrial revolution changed the local marketplace by introducing big business and flooding the market with manufactured goods. You could be successful in this environment by leveraging relationships and simply taking customer orders. Next we discovered need-satisfaction selling. Buyers have pain and sales reps show how their solution eases the pain.

Then along came the Internet, social media, and global competition. You could no longer just "propose and close" or depend on a relationship to win. You had to add significant value to the sale process or risk being replaced by a streamlined, lower cost supply chain.

Customers today are better educated, better informed, better trained and have higher expectations from the people who call on them. They are engaged with social media and they do their research on you personally through LinkedIn and your company through Facebook, your company's website, third-party websites providing reviews, bookmarking sites, and other social media tools such as blogs.

Your customers are also paying more attention to return on investment (ROI) and differentiating the value of the products and services they purchase. Your customers expect you to listen to their specific needs, offer some insight into their business and partner with them to tailor your solution or create a new one. They expect you to educate them about opportunities flowing from your insights. They expect your company to collaborate with them and innovate in designing products and services to capture new opportunities. In other words, they expect you to take a consultative approach to selling.

CHAPTER 2:
WHAT CUSTOMERS WANT

*Earn the Right to Close
through Understanding*

Today your customers are 58% of the way through their buying process before contact with a sales person, according to an IBM study. Your customers expect that you should know your company, its products and your industry. By keeping your customers up to date on industry issues, you reinforce your position as a consultative sales person, and reassure your customers that they are doing business with the best company available. Your customers expect you to be familiar with their company, especially if they are a leader in their industry or a prominent company in the local community.

Become a trusted information source by regularly posting on social media sites third-party articles, blog entries and studies that speak to the pain points and desires of potential customers. Also, interact with connections by commenting on their observations and answering their questions. Also, join industry-related groups and interact. If you do this in the service of your customer you will become a *Trusted Advis*or.

Your customers want you to be authentic in your dealings with them. Figure 1 below shows how consultative selling and the traditional "hard sell" compare on values and methods.

Feature	Consultative Selling	Traditional Selling
Values	Integrity Respect for the customer Authentic communication Sincerity Education	Expediency Arrogance Manipulation Deception "Spin"
Competencies	Listening Probing for needs Creative problem-solving Innovation Trust.-building Assertiveness Persistence	Fast-talking Probing for weaknesses Creative trickery Control Bullying, nagging, manipulation Pushy
Orientation	Customer needs and opportunities The customer is educated to make an informed buying decision	Product promises The customer is pressured into the sale
Motivation	Service to others	Greed
Strategy	Find customer-partners Under promise, over deliver Lengthy sales cycle	Target the vulnerable Over promise, under deliver One call sale
Tactics	Build credibility and mutual respect, understand customer needs and goals, uncover new opportunities, find mutually beneficial solutions and gain agreement to action plans	Impress the customer; play on fears or greed; push the product on the customer; make him take it; get the money; move onto the next prospect
Measures of Success	Multiple: including customer loyalty, profit., community respect, employee satisfaction	Singular; profit.

Figure 1: Consultative versus Traditional Selling. *Customers today respond best to a consultative approach to selling*

The hard-sell approach may work with some customers but at a price too high for many customers.

Developing a Consultative Approach to Selling

The buying process for large ticket items in most companies is complex and lengthy, increasingly requiring teams to do the buying. Your job is to see to it that these key players get answers to their questions and concerns. Figure 2 below shows the requirements and psychological needs of the players on your customer's team and your approach to them.

Player	Business Requirements	Psychological Needs	Your Approach
Sponsor	Find a suitable business partner	Recognition	Give them the credit for a successful outcome; thank them for their confidence in you; communicate in writing and in person your appreciation for the work it took to prepare and manage the buying team. With their permission, highlight them personally in your company newsletters and customer case studies. Invite them as special guests or as speakers at company or industry events.
End-user	Ease of use Effectiveness Reliability Customer support	Respect	Provide "hands-on" opportunities for them; validate their business needs and give them the operational information they require.
Purchasing Manager	Value Terms Warranty Budget ROI Risk management	Reassurance; Purchasing Managers are often at the bottom of the totem pole and crave respect.	Prove the value of your solution with hard data. Calculate ROI. Schedule the investment installments, accrued savings and/or revenue/productivity benefits. Identify and mitigate risks. Introduce them to your senior managers.
Project Manager	Scalability Interoperability Integration Installation timeframe Support	Control	Provide installation and implementation schedules. Identify key milestones. Describe how your solution fits the big picture. Provide case studies of successful installations and customer testimonials. Provide your company's org chart, showing customer support. Introduce them to your company's senior managers. Allow them to make choices during your sales presentations. Provide product/solution options.

| Technical Expert | Quality and Reliability | Recognition | Provide technical data related to quality and reliability, testimonials and case studies focusing on technical issues. Invite their questions, validate their concerns and issues and link them to experts on your sales team. |

Figure 2: Strategies for Five Kinds of Buyers *Your sales strategy must take into account the business and psychological needs of decision makers and those who influence them.*

You must first view the world from your customers' chair before presenting your solution. Your customers are motivated by *pleasure,* the opportunities that they are trying to capture, or by *pain,* the worry items that keep them awake at night. Your customer has two to five business and/or psychological needs which are the most pressing. Your customer may also have *wants,* which often look and sound like needs but turn out to be unnecessary for a sale.

Giving Customers What They Want

Sometimes you must give your customer what they want, and not what they need. In many cases, your customer's business requirements are the most important driver in the buying decision. Even if the decision is based primarily on emotion (e.g., your customer loves your high-tech gadgets), the decision typically has to be justified or rationalized with a business case that withstands inspection by other executives.

Your customer's business requirements are SPACED:

- **S**afety—how safe is the solution? What is the potential for failure? What are the side effects of the solution? Will the solution create more or tougher problems than it solves?

- **P**erformance—does the solution work, will it solve the problem in the way your customer has prescribed or the way you have claimed?

- **A**ssurance—does the solution meet the quality standards specified by your customer for such things as performance, appearance, form, fit, functionality, reliability and speed?

- **Customer service**—will you stand behind the solution? What are the service promises and how well will you meet them?

- **Efficiency**—are the alleged benefits derived from the solution worth the cost? Are there hidden costs or potential adverse impacts that may occur?

- **Delivery**—will the installation of the solution fit in the necessary time window? Will the major milestones be met? How will installation or operation of the solution affect the day-to-day operations?

Understanding Hidden Business Needs

Important business needs are often hidden. What you see is just the tip of the iceberg. Uncover these needs through building trust, listening and asking questions. Sometimes when customers think that their business requirements and/or psychological needs might not be met, they express their concerns directly to you and suggest that you collaborate with them to analyze and solve the problem.

How Your Customer Manages Supplier Relationships

As downsizing and outsourcing continue customers are adopting systems and processes to manage the increasing number and variety of suppliers. At first you are simply another *Bidder* to them. If you meet their standards of quality service and price, then they see you as a *Supplier*. If you are successful in winning more business and if you replicate your earlier success a number of times, you may become a *Preferred Supplier*. If you continue to provide value, and demonstrate increasing knowledge of your customers' business, your customers may take you into their confidence and ask you to *solve problems* for them without subjecting you to a competitive process. Finally, if you perform the problem-solver role exceptionally well by demonstrating insight, innovation and value, and building trusting relationships at every level of your customers' organization, your customer may invite you to the status of *Partner*. Figure 3 illustrates this hierarchy.

Partnership is the Goal, or is It?

Your ultimate goal in sales is to create a portfolio of profitable customers who are intensely loyal to you and who regularly send you referrals. Figure 3 below shows the results of various approaches to your account list.

If Your Approach is to	Your Customer Will See You As a	Resulting in
Identify/solve problems, educate and create opportunities	Partner	High revenue high profit
Respond to customer-identified problems	Problem Solver	High revenue, moderate profit
Perform well repeatedly	Preferred Supplier	Moderate revenue, moderate profit
Quote and hope	Supplier	Low revenue, low profit
Bid and buy	Bidder	Low revenue, low profit

Figure 3: Step Up to Partner. *Attain the financial rewards you want by changing your sales approach*

To retain partnership status with your customer you must invest considerable time and effort in nurturing the relationship and learning about the opportunities and challenges your partner faces.

CHAPTER 3:
PROSPECTING FOR NEW CUSTOMERS

If you're not enthusiastic about your value proposition, how can you expect your customer to be?

Research indicates that only about 15% of leads are immediately willing to buy. Approximately 20% are disqualified initially, leaving 65% with varying levels of interest. The task now is to stay in touch with this 65%, so that when it's time to make a buying decision, the prospect remembers your brand. Also, the Sales Benchmark Index found that 58% of the pipeline stalls, because the sales person has not presented enough value to keep the sale moving.

From your perspective the sales cycle consists of:

- Prospecting
- Qualifying
- Fact and feeling finding
- Preparing and presenting a proposal
- Overcoming objections
- Closing

However this is not your customers' view of the process. For starters, your customers call it a "buying" not a "selling" process and see themselves as the owner, managing objectives and activities to select the best supplier. They also involve more stakeholders in the buying process. A 2012 survey of B2B buyers conducted by Demand Gen Report found that 50% more decision makers seek the input of more internal members during the decision making process, compared to 30% of buyers surveyed in 2011.

The stages in the customer buying process are:

- Developing the specifications for the product/service solution and the criteria for selecting a supplier
- Confirming the budget
- Assessing the capabilities of suppliers
- Distributing a formal or informal request for proposal (RFP) to qualified suppliers
- Selecting finalists from proposals and inviting them to make a presentation with a question-and-answer session
- Selecting a winner.

Figure 4 below illustrates and compares the processes.

The buying processes for the most part mirrors the sales cycle. At decision points, you should summarize where you both are, ask if your customer is ready to move forward to the next stage and then suggest what that might be. Do not dictate next steps to your customer, nor passively allow your customer to tell you what to do.

Buying Process					
Developing specs	Qualifying suppliers	Distributing RFP to qualified suppliers	Inviting finalists to make a presentation	Question-and-answer session	Selecting a winner
Prospecting	Qualifying prospects	Information Gathering	Preparing and delivering a proposal	Overcoming objections	Closing
Selling Process					

Figure 4: The Buying /Selling Processes Mirror Each Other. *Respect your customers' desire to manage their sales process by suggesting limited choices for next steps.*

Prospecting is the first step in your sales process, and no matter how good a sales person you are, is a step that you cannot skip for any significant length of time. Prospecting is the process of identifying and attracting suspects. A *suspect* is someone who appears to fit your target market, for example, retail businesses with less than $25 million a year in volume in the 14607 zip code, or shows some interest in you, your products or your company. A qualified *prospect* is someone who has the Money, the Authority and the Desire (MAD) to buy your products.

A *Customer* is someone who buys from you – once. A *Friend* is someone who buys from you more than once. And an *Advocate* is a customer who buys repeatedly from you and sends you referrals. And referrals are your best source of new business.

Generating Leads

The process of converting suspects to prospects, prospects to customers, customers to friends and friends to advocates is called *the sales pipeline, sales cycle or sales funnel*. View prospecting as an integral part of your sales pipeline. Make friends with marketing. It is their job to generate leads. However, you must also do your own prospecting.

Generate your own leads through speaking at industry events, conducting a webinar, doing your own email blast, asking your best customers for referrals, writing a newsletter or blog, engaging suspects in a conversation on social media and cold calling. Experiment to see which combination works best for you. Remember to coordinate with marketing so that your prospects hear you as one voice.

Start a conversation with prospects on Twitter, LinkedIn or other sites. Your immediate objective is to generate interest, not to inform the customer of your products' features. Set goals for yourself to trigger the self-fulfilling prophecy phenomenon. Increase your prospecting not out of fear, not in a panicky, impulsive flurry of phone calls, but in a confident, methodical way.

Creating a Sense of Urgency

Reach out to new people every single day - no matter what. No one ever gets too successful to prospect. It's quite the opposite; daily commitment to prospecting is what makes long term success possible. Begin to create a sense of urgency as you prospect. Momentum and a sense of urgency are necessary conditions for closing sales, and it starts with your first contact with your prospect. Remember that your goal for the initial phone call is to get an appointment. In most cases you need to be face-to-face with your prospect to make a consultative sale. For example,

"Mr. /Ms. Prospect, we have a new/updated/revolutionary/breakthrough/ unique/ (creates urgency) idea/program/concept/solution/system (never "a product") that will save you money/make you money/improve productivity. (Benefit) I'm offering you an opportunity today to evaluate/see for yourself/judge for yourself/determine (you are in control, Ms. Prospect.) whether or not it will be of benefit and value to you. (Answers the question "*What's In It for Me?" (WIIFM*)). Our senior account exec/director of sales/customer relationship manager (never a "sales rep"; this is much too important) will be in your area tomorrow (not a week from Friday. This is urgent!) Are you in at 7 AM or 8 AM tomorrow?" (Not "when will you be available tomorrow?". Stress urgency again).

Door-Openers

Referrals are one of your prime sources of new business. A warm referral increases the odds of a sales success two to four times (Opportunities to Profit from Social Selling, CustomerThink).

The *Endorsement* approach: Nothing works like a referral from a friend, colleague, or even a competitor.

You: "Good morning, Ms. Smith. This is Tom Chang of Universal Systems. One of your associates, Brenda Beeline, suggested that you might be interested in some ideas to manage your inventory."

The *Limited Opportunity* approach: A deadline, limited offers, once-in-a-lifetime opportunity presents a strong motivator.

You: "Hello, Mr. Rodriguez, this is Fiona Fortune of American Software. We're running a special sale on software upgrades that I know you'll want to take advantage of. The sale ends at 5 o'clock this afternoon."

The *Special Fact* approach: News about your customer's business is attention getting.

You: "Good morning, Mr. Washington. This is Eric Expediter of On Time Limousine Service. I just received the results of a limousine usage study of companies like yours."

The *Special Offer* approach

You: "This month, you'll get an additional six-month service warranty free." Or, "If you order a 12-month supply, we'll defer billing for 60 days."

The *Survey* approach

You: "Your industry's association reported that almost 61 percent of the companies surveyed had problems with over-inventory. What is your experience?"

In pulling together your sales message, choose between a script and a prompt guide, depending on your comfort level.

Enter results in your contact management software program and continue calling each day until contact is made. Persistence counts. According to a recent National Sales Executive Association survey, 80 percent of all new sales are made at the fifth contact with the same prospect.

Cold Calling

Cold calling is the process of approaching suspects, typically via telephone, who have not agreed to such an interaction. Cold calling that enables you to call without being rejected is based on the idea that the purpose of the call is not to make a sale, but to build trust and discover the truth about whether there is a good match between the suspect and your product or service. It works best when you lay the groundwork for your call through emails and/or social media contact.

Prospecting by the Numbers

Set aside at least an hour a day for prospecting. Segment your accounts by grouping them according to geography, industry or size. Construct a customer-centered *value proposition* that uncovers a problem in their industry that may not be recognized. (For how to do this, see Chapter 7, Preparing and Presenting your Proposal). Aim for 50 - 75 phone calls a day. Expect to reach 6-8 qualified prospects a day. You goal is to make appointments with 50%, or 4 prospects and close 25% of those. For most industries, there are similar sales ratios to work with. Stay in touch with prospects over a long sales cycle through web conferences that update customers on industry news, product changes, certification issues, pricing changes or promotions.

Setting Call Objectives

Before every sales call, on the telephone or in the field, do some background research on your prospect or customer. Prepare call objectives, questions, sales aids and coach technical experts or other team members. Prepare also ideas or value propositions to present. Calculate expected sales call outcomes.

To prepare for each call, begin by setting call objectives. Incorporate phrases that intrigue and hold your customer's attention.

You: "Ms. Customer, the purpose of today's meeting is for you to evaluate how our portfolio of products and services support your department's policy-making, and executive decisions. To recap, as you suggested, we surveyed your key executives to determine their current sources of economic and political information. We reviewed the results with you and identified where decision-support information appeared to be less than adequate. Based on that analysis we have prepared some pre-proposal recommendations which we will share with you today. Is this more or less what you expected to have happen today?"

You will get objections to closing on the appointment. Here are a few:

Example 1

Customer: "Send me some information first."

You: "I can do one better than that. One of the product developers, Karen Anderson, will be in Detroit tomorrow, so she can walk you through the information personally. Will you be in around 3:30 PM?"

Example 2

Customer: "Now is a bad time."

You: "I certainly appreciate how valuable your time is Mr. Inactive Account. On the other hand, it will only take you five minutes to see if we have anything of benefit or value for you. What would be easiest, tomorrow morning or afternoon?"

Example 3

Customer: "We had record sales last year. We don't need your _____."

You: "That is exactly why I called you. Some of our best customers are exceptionally successful, and in part, it is because they are continuously raising the bar. They take advantage of new ideas to make the small changes that keep them just that much better than the competition. You will know in the first five minutes if we can improve your operation. How's tomorrow, first thing?"

Example 4

Customer: "Have no budget."

You; "I met with a (insert prospects industry here) company recently. They had some pretty good plans in place already, and what budget they had was fully allocated. Because they like to keep abreast of the industry, they agreed to meet us for just a few minutes. The manager was so impressed with what he heard that he immediately scheduled a meeting for us with some key colleagues. No commitments of course, but clearly they could see real value in exploring fresh ideas."

Example 5

Customer: "Give me some more info first."

You: "What would you like to know?"

Customer: "Well, what is this model/system? Has it been applied to our industry? What kind of ROI is it getting? I've got a million questions."

You: "I'd be happy to explain to you on the phone but I'm not sure I could do justice to your questions. I guarantee you'll be impressed with our solution within the first few minutes of our meeting. Tomorrow, late morning, or early afternoon?"

Qualifying Prospects

A critical objective in prospecting is qualifying, which determines if a person who has shown some interest in your value proposition has the potential to become a customer. *Suspects* therefore, are potential buyers who have not yet been qualified. Time invested in listening for needs, preparing and presenting a proposal is wasted if your suspect is not qualified (for example, has no budget). In addition to the time savings, there are always hard costs involved in working a suspect through the sales cycle. With a well-qualified suspect, the chances of a win are significantly better, and your morale remains high. As the trend towards team-based organization structures and outsourcing to preferred partners continues, qualifying your suspect becomes more complex.

Are they MAD?

Your qualifying objective is to determine your suspect's level of interest in your company's capabilities or value proposition. Your suspect's Desire falls into one of two categories – pain or pleasure. Here are some qualifying questions for *Desire*.

Goals

- What are your top three business goals for this year?
- How important are these goals to your company's growth plans?
- How do they support the company's growth strategy?
- What happens to managers at your company who achieve or exceed their goals?
- What happens if you do not achieve these goals?
- How does this project fit into your business plans?

Attempted Solutions

- What are some of the solutions you have tried in the past (or currently using)?
- What results did you get?
- Were those results acceptable?
- What kinds of solutions are you considering this time?
- What results do you expect?
- What thoughts do you have about measuring results?
- What other methods did you consider to achieve your goals?
- Are you open to considering some creative ideas?

Your Competition

- What other firms/suppliers are you talking to?
- Do you have a specific proposal from them?
- What is in it?
- What criteria are you going to use to select a partner?
- Which criterion is the most important to you?
- Do we have a shot at this?

Final Question

- Is there anything else you think I should know about your plans?

The next qualifying criterion is Authority, which means determining who in your suspect's organization would sign-off on your proposal. Here are some examples of questions that probe the *Authority* issues.

Authority Questions

- What is the decision-making process for this project?
- Who else do you need to consult before making a decision?

- Is there anyone else you think I should talk to about this project?

- Whose head will roll if this project is not a success?

Last Question

- Is there anything else you think I should know about your decision-making process?

Determine if your suspect has a budget for the project, and if not, how your suspect intends to fund it. You must also identify who in your suspect organization will authorize the expenditure. Here are some questions that help qualify a suspect on the *Money* criterion.

Budget Size

- Whose budget is this coming out of?

- How much have you set-aside for this project?

- How are you proposing to fund the project?

- Are there any other projects competing for these dollars?

Budget Process

- What is your company's process for funding these types of investments?

- When does the budget process begin?

- What are the steps in your budgeting process?

Last Question

- Is there anything else you think I should know about your budget?

The result of probing is that you convert a cool, unknown suspect to a warm, qualified prospect.

CHAPTER 4:
LISTENING TO CUSTOMER NEEDS

Improve your listening by taking the cotton out of your ears and putting it in your mouth.

Listening to customer needs means communicating your understanding back to your customer in a way that deepens your customer's awareness and understanding of their needs and moves the sale forward. Use listening to qualify your customers, to make a bid/no bid decisions, to overcome objections and to negotiate win/win agreements

Example

Customer:	"Our CEO has three key initiatives this year that involve coordinated, cross-department service delivery. We have never done that before, and we have never had such an aggressive implementation timetable. So if your company has a new, breakthrough software solution…"
You:	"That depends, Jose. What is your role in this initiative?"
Customer:	"I'm the guy the CEO appointed to make this happen. I'm heading up a cross departmental, cross-functional planning and implementation team. For me, this is a significant project."
You:	"How significant, Jose?"
Customer:	"It's a high visibility, high value project. If it's a success, I'll be a hero."
You:	"And if it fails..?"

Customer: "Well, let's just say that I'll have plenty of time for sailing."

To listen effectively, you must remain detached and dispassionate about your own emotions or they'll interfere with your ability to hear what's really being said. Never make your customers feel that they are being interrogated.

Listening and Probing Go Hand in Hand

The secret to drawing a person out is to use open-ended rather than closed-ended questions. Having asked that initial open-ended question and gotten the prospect talking, you'll want to keep probing and clarifying, but not in a way that stops the flow. Listen some more to your sales call with your customer, Jose.

You: "Sounds like a wonderful opportunity, Jose, and also a lot of pressure. How will you measure success?"

Customer: "Two ways. We've got to be able to show cost savings of x million dollars and we have to hit every milestone on our launch and delivery timetable."

You: "And what do you anticipate will be the biggest obstacle to success?"

Customer: "You mean besides me and my big mouth?.... I'd say getting everyone on the same page. The people on my team are all senior executives with their own high priority projects. I don't know where some of them are going to find the time for my project."

You: "I'm beginning to see the picture. Sounds like you really have your hands full. The more I hear the more confident I am that we can offer you and your team a system and tools that will save time in coordinating the implementation. As well as project and track cost savings. Interested?"

Customer: "Maybe. Show me how it works."

LISTENING TO CUSTOMER NEEDS

Note the listening, clarifying and probing sequence in this sales dialogue.

You: "I'm confused, Ellen. This morning you emphasized that you need flexibility. As you nicely put it, you want your technology to support people and change, not the other way around. With a fixed-price contract, your suppliers will be forced to increase their prices to cover the inflation risk, which means that you might not realize the long term cost savings you want. Are you open to alternative financing?"

Customer: "I doubt it. The cost savings are critical for us, and a fixed price contract benefits you too. This is a win-win provision."

You: "Would you be prepared to trade-off cost savings for flexibility?"

Customer: "Your proposal must address both cost savings and flexibility, while supporting people."

You: "OK, I'm trying to put myself in your shoes. I want to know that I'm paying less for the next five years than I'm currently paying. At the same time, I want a solution flexible enough to adapt to change, while supporting people. Ellen, what do you mean by "supporting people"?

Customer: "Perhaps "supporting" is not quite the right word. Perhaps, "user-friendly technology" is a more accurate descriptor. We want the technology to adapt to change but we don't want to burden our people with unnecessary, "whistles and bells," and we don't want them to spend long periods of time in the classroom learning new applications every time a change comes along. They are stressed enough already."

You: "Right. So you will want a relationship with a partner who understands your changing needs, who can perhaps anticipate changes, who can help you manage the changes, and be especially sensitive to the impact of the changes on people. Am I on target?"

Converting suspects to prospects, prospects to customers, customers to friends and friends to advocates requires accurate and empathic listening and laser-like probing. Similarly, listen for your customer's perspective on the problem and be aware that perspectives may vary. Your ability to take your customer's perspective communicates your flexibility, intelligence, and your respect for your customer, which builds trust and leads to more business.

Removing Barriers to Listening

Customers may put up barriers to listening. They mumble, don't complete sentences, express ideas poorly, use distracting mannerisms, have negative or condescending attitudes towards you, or even a hostile or intimidating demeanor. As a result you focus on the barriers instead of the message and consequently miss or distort your customer's message.

Barriers that you can do something about are those you put up yourself. Eliminate distractions in your work environment. You may get turned off by your customer's personality, offensive remarks, or critical comments made about your company. Monitor and manage your feelings to mitigate against under or over reacting to your customer.

You avoid many barriers to effective listening by simply taking an active, positive role. Take notes; it makes you listen.

Paraphrasing your Customers' Message

Paraphrasing is a listening skill that you use to ensure that you have heard what your customer intended you to hear, to buy yourself time to recover from a failed tactic, to regain control of your sales call, to interrupt a customer who is repetitive or aimless and to reassure your customer that you grasp their key message.

Example

You: "Mr. Customer, you mentioned supplier problems earlier. What happened exactly?"

Customer: "They just don't get it. They quickly respond to all our service requests, including outages and requests for upgrades, but they don't see the big picture. They have made no attempt to analyze the patterns of service complaints and email usage. They have not proposed changes at the systemic level. They are nice people, but we have outgrown them. They were shocked when I announced I was putting together a RFP."

You: "So you are looking for a partner who can not only propose the best solution, but also one who is proactive, and can feed you ideas and alert you to issues. Am I right?"

Customer: "You are right on, though you probably won't find it put quite so clearly in the RFP."

Listening with Empathy

Empathy is the ability to put yourself in the shoes of your customer and experience events and emotions the way they do. Being empathetic requires that you momentarily put aside your agenda, your thoughts and feelings, let your guard down and "put yourself in the shoes" of your customer without attempting to judge or problem-solve it. Empathy is a gift – a gift of yourself at a point in time to your customer. Women are conditioned to be more empathic than men, but men can learn to improve their empathy with their customers.

Example

Customer: "Our current email system is nuts. For starters, we've got too many unnecessary mail boxes. Even the janitors have mail boxes! The system is painfully slow and we have had too many outages. It has limited remote access capability. Some departments have bought upgrades, their own anti-spam and anti-pop-up applications, and the entire system, if you can call it a system that runs off 37 different servers! Can you believe that! 37! We even found one server in a coat closet!"

You: "Sounds like you are really frustrated with it. (Customer nods, eyes downcast) What have you done so far to fix it?"

Example

You: "You are still not comfortable with it, are you? I can understand your reluctance. I sit in your office and tell you that we can do this project for you, I show you a letter from a customer, but those nagging doubts are still there, aren't they." (Arms still crossed, customer shrugs apologetically.)

Making the effort to develop and apply your empathy enables you and your customer to understand your customer's business and psychological needs and collaborate in developing a solution.

CHAPTER 5:
CONVERTING PROSPECTS TO CUSTOMERS

"Collecting data is like collecting garbage. Pretty soon, we have to do something with it."
-Mark Twain

When you have separated the suspects from the prospects you are ready to move into the most critical part of the sales cycle: sorting suspects from prospects through the qualifying process. Time invested in listening for needs, preparing and presenting a proposal can be completely wasted if your suspect is not qualified (for example, has no budget). In addition to the time savings, there are always hard costs involved in converting suspects to advocates. As the trend towards team-based organization structures and outsourcing to preferred partners continues, qualifying your suspect becomes more complex.

Converting Suspects to Prospects; are they MAD?

Qualified prospects, also known as "hot" prospects, are potential customers who have the *Money, Authority and Desire (MAD)* to buy from you. Until you have established that they meet all three of the MAD criteria, they are simply suspects. Suspects are potential customers who meet at least one of the MAD criteria.

Benefits of Qualifying

Control the sales process by qualifying suspects. Asking questions gives you control. Answering questions loses control. Save time and money by qualifying. Qualifying makes your job easier. When you qualify a suspect, you are simplifying and focusing your sales efforts. Qualifying paves the way for partners.

Probing is the Key Skill

The main skill you need for qualifying is the probe. *Probing* means digging below the surface and uncovering unspoken needs. Often good probes raise more questions than they answer. Use *Follow-Up Probes* to get all the information you need, including information that is hidden, contradictory, confusing, alluded to, secret or sensitive.

Probe wide and probe deep to get the full picture. Ask "Why..?" five times to uncover the real reason for a customer's statement. The following example demonstrates the basic process:

You: "Why the expanded operations specs? They exceed your current requirements."

Customer: "We just want to be sure we have adequate capacity."

You: "Why?"

Customer: "Well we might want to expand operations at some point."

You: "Why?"

Customer: "The market is changing and we expect to find ourselves in a growth situation."

You: "Why?"

Customer: (Pause.) "Well, you never know, we might acquire our major competitor."

You: "Why?"

Customer: "They are weak in operations, which is our strength. They are strong in marketing, which is not our strength. If we acquire them, there's going to be a lot more opportunities for you guys."

Gathering Information

In the process of qualifying your prospect and in subsequent sales calls you begin to gather information you need to put together a presentation and/or a proposal. Probe wide and probe deep. Below are some examples.

- What prompted you/ your company to look into this?
- What are your expectations/ requirements for this product/ service?
- What process did you go through to determine your needs?
- How do you see this happening?
- What is it that you'd like to see accomplished?
- With whom have you had success in the past?
- With whom have you had difficulties in the past?
- Can you help me understand that a little better?
- What does that mean?
- How does that process work now?
- What challenges does that process create?
- What challenges has that created in the past?
- How did you resolve them in the past?
- What are the best things about that process?
- What other items should we discuss?

Prepare for information gathering by organizing your planned probes into categories. Figure 6, below, shows sample categories and probes.

Mission and Goals	Quality	Service
What are your customer's mission, vision and values? Customer's growth strategy for the next 12 months? How do our products/services support their strategy?	What quality standards do they expect? Have they registered complaints with us?	What service standards do they expect?
Competition	History	Decision Making
Are we a sole source? What percent? What is the market price for products/services like ours?	Order history, volumes, products, prices Customer satisfaction Our relationship with key people	What is the decision making process? Who are the stakeholders in decisions? Who else influences decisions? Who are your advocates? Are there any against you or the project?
Culture	Legal Issues	Industry Trends
Do we understand what is "normal" negotiating? Understand what is and is not socially acceptable for the culture?	Liability Non complete, exclusivity agreements Rights to use of brands Taxes and duties	What are the current trends in the customers industry?

Figure 6: Organize your Information Gathering. *You will get all the information you need to create a winning proposal by following this systematic and thorough approach to your sales calls.*

To ensure full cooperation from your customer organization and to impress on decision-makers and decision-influencers your professionalism, be sure that while information gathering, take the time to build some rapport and point out how their answers benefit their company. At the end of the interview, ask the customer if they have any questions for you, thank them for the information, leave your business card in case they think of something later and exit promptly.

Avoid these Probes

Some types of probes you should avoid because they are ineffective or inefficient. *Doubles* are two probes joined by an "and" or a pause, which could confuse your customer. For example, "How's that report working out for you and did you see the table on page seven?" *Multiple Choice* is a set of closed-ended probes, which may not cover all the possible cases. For example, "Did you not like our service or was it the price or did you find someone else?" A *Convoluted* probe is straightforward with an unnecessary preamble. For example, "Now I know you guys have an awful lot on your plate at the moment and you are not alone by the way. All my customers are feeling the pressure, and you have probably told me this before so forgive me for asking again, but what is the deadline for proposals?" *Judgmental* probes may appear to place you in a position of superiority over your customer and can be offensive. "Doesn't that seem like a waste of time?" sounds arrogant and tactless to a customer who has spent several minutes proudly telling you about his plans. *Jargon* is terminology, much like slang, that relates to a specific activity, profession or group. It often comes across as pedantic, nerdy, and divorced from meaning to outsiders. It's best to avoid it unless you have heard your customer use it correctly herself. *Leading* probes are intended to gather objective information but have a definite bias to them. For example, "Would you describe your current process as inefficient?"

Think about the qualifying process as a search for a partner to do business with.

Building Rapport with Customers

Building rapport means establishing a connection between you and your suspect so that they can feel that you are like them in some way and can trust you. Gentle teasing is effective in disarming a customer and revealing more of your personality.

Example

Customer: "Here's my business card."

You: (Glancing at the job title) "How long have you been in this position, Mr. Customer?"

Customer: "Let's see…about 18 months I guess."

You: (Grinning) "Got the hang of it yet?" (Customer laughs)

Building rapport means establishing a connection between you and your customer so that they can feel that you are like them in some way. Here are some tips.

- Introduce self (company and team)
- Use customer's name early and often
- Shake hands at every opportunity
- Use simple, persuasive words
- Make eye contact, smile
- Look for areas of mutual interest
- Show genuine interest in the other person
- Share the authentic you
- Break the ice with laughter
- Be polite, respectful
- Maintain a positive attitude - everybody loves a winner
- Avoid discussing politics, religion, sex, drugs until you have built a very strong relationship

Earning your Customer's Trust

If your customers perceive you as like them in some way, no matter how insignificant it may seem, they are more likely to trust you. Understanding your customer's buying style and flexing to it helps build a trusting relationship with your customer.

Making the Conscious Decision to Pursue

Make the decision to pursue a qualified prospect a conscious one. Beware of falling into the trap of going to the next step without evaluating the opportunity. You will have prospects that are qualified but may not be worth pursuing. The decision to pursue or not pursue is aimed at eliminating opportunities that you have a low probability of winning. Improving bid discipline can double or triple your win rate, and improving the quality of your proposals can improve your win rate by 15 to 20 percent. A "no-pursuit" decision does not mean a lost prospect.

CHAPTER 6:
READING CUSTOMER BUYING STYLES

Customers buy from people they perceive to be like them in some way.

The way your customers prefer to manage their relationships with you is determined to some extent by their buying style. Your customer's *buying style* is his or her habitual, non-verbal communication with you, determined by his or her personality and buying experiences. In a similar way, your *selling style* influences the way you prefer to manage your sales relationships. Your *selling style* is your habitual, non-verbal communication with customers, determined by your personality and your sales experiences. You can improve your communication with your customers, avoid misunderstandings and conflicts, and build trusting relationships by simply understanding your customers' buying style and adjusting yours.

Analyzing your Customer's Buying Style

Understand your customer's buying style by first determining if they appear to be more comfortable being outgoing or reserved. Outgoing customers tend to talk more than they listen, make statements more than they ask questions, use frequent gestures, are proactive, usually have a moderate to high energy level and tend to "think out aloud." Reserved customers are the opposite. They tend to be quiet, passive, observant, still and inscrutable. They ask thoughtful questions and do not usually share much about themselves or their ideas unless called upon. Your customer probably falls somewhere in between these two types because, in fact, they are on a continuum. Try and locate them predominantly at one end or the other. Your customer will probably behave according to the demands of the situation, making your determination about their style preference more challenging. For example, reserved and outgoing customers may lead a meeting in a similar, professional manner requiring that you look for subtleties to determine their style.

Next, determine if your customer prefers the company of people or tasks. People-oriented customers tend to seek others out and enjoy their company, are sensitive to the feelings of others, get much of their information about the world and draw their inspiration and energy from other people. Task-oriented customers see the world as data, processes and things, drawing their energy and inspiration from performing tasks and problem-solving. They tend to view people as sources of data or "things" to work with. This does not mean that they are not capable of being sensitive to people, because they are usually observant and interested in what makes people tick, though from a scientific/engineering viewpoint. Your determinations should now fall neatly into the Analyzer, Driver, Supporter or Influencer boxes illustrated in Figure 7.

	Task Oriented		
Reserved	ANALYZER	DRIVER	Outgoing
	SUPPORTER	INFLUENCER	
	People Oriented		

Figure 7: Customer Buying Styles and Sales Rep Selling Styles. *Close more deals by flexing your style to your customer's.*

Identifying the Analyzer Buying Style (Task oriented and Reserved)

The Analyzers' buying decisions are logical and systematic, focused on data and facts, and conducted in a deliberate and objective manner. They respect sales reps who are knowledgeable and professional and who complete all paperwork thoroughly and accurately. They dislike being forced to make buying decisions, without adequate time, information and resources. They respond to and expect diplomacy, consideration, and respect for others. They resist having solutions forced on them - they want the data so that they can figure things out themselves. Emotionally uncontrolled situations make them very uncomfortable. During sales calls, Analyzers typically ask technical and thought-provoking questions about quality control.

The Analyzer's office is work-oriented, showing much activity and displays of achievement awards on the wall. They dress conservatively and make steady eye contact from an expressionless face. They choose their words carefully, speaking in a soft voice and pausing before speaking. Analyzers movements are controlled and formal, with minimal use of gestures.

Analyzers Favorite Sayings

- nothing but the best
- there's nothing new under the sun
- proof of concept
- quality is - job#1
- an air-tight case
- are there any other options?
- it's not who you know, it's what you know
- drill down
- no pain, no gain
- analysis paralysis
- make the case for
- solid as a rock
- substantive and sustainable change
- research-proven and field-tested

Selling to the Analyzer Style

Approach

- Be logical, organized and patient
- Slow it down
- Get right down to business
- Be deliberate, methodical
- Show proof for each claim
- Support your customer's principles
- Talk about documented facts

Analyzers prefer sales calls that allow adequate time for in-depth discussion and analysis, contain proposals that are concrete, factual and well-documented and are conducted in a low-key, private but not too personal environment.

Identifying the Supporter Buying Style
(People oriented and Reserved)

The Supporters decision-making tends to be personal in nature, focused on teamwork at a measured pace. They respect people who show loyalty and appreciation, and demonstrate sincerity and concern. They dislike change, uncertainty, disorganization, interpersonal conflict, and sales calls with large groups. They typically ask about people, processes and profit, and why you believe your company is their best choice.

The Supporter's work space is warm, comfortable and inviting, displaying pictures of family and personal mementos. They tend to wear comfortable, casual and conservative clothing. Supporters will greet you with natural, warm eye contact, a pleasant and attentive smile and a warm, clasping handshake. Supporters speak slowly and calmly in soothing voices and move about gracefully.

Supporter's Favorite Sayings

- empowering
- form follows function
- what goes around comes around
- a journey of a thousand miles begins with one step
- involve all our stakeholders
- heartfelt
- there's no "I" in team
- none of us is as smart as all of us
- ready, aim, fire
- measure twice, cut once

Selling to the Supporter Style
(People oriented and Reserved)

Approach

- Be supportive
- Slow it down
- Get to know them, talk about personal life; be sociable
- Project warmth and sincerity
- Seek common areas of interest or backgrounds
- Communicate informally and casually
- Your solution should minimize the level of risk - Typically they are not risk takers.

Supporters prefer sales calls that take into account the involvement of others, follow a standard process, and propose conservative, proven solutions to problems.

Identifying the Driver Buying Style (Task oriented and Assertive)

The Drivers' decision-making tends to be forceful and competitive, quick-paced, decisive and results oriented. They respect sales people who give direct answers and meet the sales challenges. They dislike poor work standards, inefficiency and slowness, and routine sales procedures. They typically ask procedural and outcome oriented questions.

The Driver's workspace is organized, neat and sparsely furnished with achievement awards on the wall.

A calendar is often prominently displayed. The Driver's desk is located between the Director's and visitor's chairs. Drivers have a business-like, conservative appearance and make Intense, steady eye contact, with limited facial expressions. Their sentences are short and the structure is clipped. They tend to speak rapidly and loudly, issuing concise directives and statements. Their gestures are controlled, punchy and deliberate with an efficiency of movement. They are fond of jabbing motions with their index finger.

The Driver's Favorite Sayings

- get results
- top priority
- deal with it
- just do it
- seal the deal
- reach our goal
- quick and dirty
- turnkey operation
- if it ain't broke don't fix it

- where the rubber meets the road
- cut to the chase
- save time
- quick wins
- a slam dunk
- a tight ship

Selling to the Driver Style

In general

- Speed it up, get to the point
- Be decisive
- Be businesslike, time conscious and factual
- Show them how to reach their goal
- Project conviction and efficiency
- Talk about immediate action
- Allow them the control they need by offering a limited number of options

Drivers prefer sales calls that are brief, to the point with a clear and obtainable objective and a one page summary of your proposal with two or three recommendations. They want very little rapport building. Notice how the sales rep matches her customer's Driver style in the following dialogue.

You: "Sounds like a wonderful opportunity, but also a lot of pressure. How will you measure success?"

Customer: "Two ways. We've got to be able to show cost savings of x million dollars and we have to hit every milestone on our launch and delivery timetable."

You: "And what do you anticipate will be the biggest obstacle to success?"

Customer: "You mean besides me and my big mouth?.... I'd say getting everyone on the same page. The people on my team are all senior executives with their own high priority projects. I don't know where some of them are going to find the time for my project."

You: "I'm beginning to see the picture. Sounds like you really have your hands full. The more I hear, the more confident I am that we can offer you and your team a system and tools that will save time in coordinating the implementation. And, project and track cost savings. Interested?"

Customer: "Maybe. Show me how it works."

You: "OK. Sure… One more, quick question. Is there funding available for this project?"

Customer: "This is the CEO's number one priority. There's plenty of money but it has not yet been allocated to specific initiatives. You make a compelling case and I'll get the money."

Identifying the Influencer Buying Style

The Influencers' decision-making style is personal and enthusiastic, quick paced, persuasive and tied to a big picture. Influencers respect sales people who collaborate with them and maintain an open mind. They typically ask who will be involved in the sales process but dislike being bogged down in details and prefer to leave the follow through to others.

The Influencer's work space is colorful and dramatic, scattered with unusual artifacts. There may be motivational pictures on the wall, the desk cluttered and messy and furniture arranged for open contact with people. They make intense, friendly but intermittent eye-contact with animated facial expressions and considerable variation in speech tone, speed and pitch. Their language tends to be rich and colorful, illustrated with frequent and expansive gestures.

The Influencer's Favorite Sayings

- they'll love it
- make boat loads of money
- do a gut check
- feels right
- keep our options open
- a world of opportunities
- it will be fun
- blue sky it
- if it ain't broke, break it
- the biggest, the best, the most
- try something new
- the 60,000 feet view
- I feel your pain
- we'll cross that bridge when we come to it
- it's not what you know it's who you know

Selling to the Influencer Style

Approach

- Explain who is involved in the sales process
- Proceed with enthusiasm and flexibility
- Support their intentions
- Talk about people and opinions
- Be entertaining and develop a personal relationship

- Avoid too much detail, but share useful ideas that can be put into action

- Maintain a warm and sociable atmosphere

Influencers prefer sales calls that describe the context or the big picture for your proposal. They look for creative ideas and innovative practices, and proposals that clearly connect to their personal agendas as well as the company's.

Flex your Style to Win over your Customer

Flexing to customer buying styles is a technique in selling which calls for you to anticipate and adapt your selling style to your customer's buying style in order to maximize your effectiveness. You should embed it in all of your sales practices. Style flexing applies to all stages of the sales process. Converting suspects to prospects, prospects to customers, customers to friends, and friends to advocates.

Flex your message to the business viewpoints of buyers, end-users, technical experts and senior managers. You must be able to see the business world through the eyes of each of these functions, and respond with the appropriate information and sales techniques. But that's not all. You must also be able to flex to the personality, buying preferences, cultural nuances and psychological needs of each of the individuals playing the functional roles. By making this connection with the customer, you enhance your chances of winning the business.

Flexing to the customer's way of buying reduces the likelihood of misunderstandings that often derail a sales effort. Buyers may reject your sales approach if they perceive you as too forceful, or not forceful enough. If you get bogged down in details, or if you don't pay enough attention to detail. If you are too passionate, or if you are not passionate enough. If you are too rigid, or if you are too loose. Understand their buying styles and flex to them. Do not ignore the cues. Monitor your responses to your customer and adjust them accordingly.

To determine how to approach each style, study the tips under each style in the text above. Use the body language cues in particular to further help identify your customer's buying style. You will probably find that you feel more comfortable with customer styles adjacent to yours. If you are a driver, for example, you'll feel more comfortable with the adjacent Analyzer style's data orientation and with the adjacent Influencer style's outgoing nature. If you are an Analyzer you'll feel comfortable with the

Driver and the Supporter and so on for the other styles. Note that you are more likely to feel challenged selling to the styles diagonally opposite to yours. If you are a free-wheeling, big-thinking Influencer you may get frustrated with an Analyzer style customer's insistence on specifics and proof that your ideas will work. On the other hand, if you're a calm, thoughtful Analyzer, you may become overwhelmed by your Influencer customer's spontaneity and innovativeness. If you are a high-energy, action and goal oriented Driver, process and people oriented Supporter customers may frustrate you with their concern for inclusion and process. If you are a sensitive, caring Supporter, you'll no doubt be sensitive to the fact that you are a minority in sales and may be appalled at your Driver customer's apparent disregard for the feelings of people. Remember, that while your opposites may challenge and even fascinate you (opposites do, after all, attract), they offer you the best opportunities to improve your all-round flexibility and sales effectiveness.

Flexing Techniques

A large part of flexing your style means imitating your customer's body language. Pace your customer's vocal style by listening to their speed, tone, volume and sentence length. Then without mimicking them, use a similar speed of voice, tone, volume and sentence length. Pacing will build rapport and establish a level of comfort for your customer.

Mirror your customer's basic gestures, expressions and body lean. Try to look more similar to than different from your customer. Position yourself similarly in terms of body lean (forward, upright, and backward) and look (casual or formal). Mirror your customer's pattern of hand gesturing but not every movement. Mirror the facial signals of smiling, attending or frowning based on the content of the message. Listen and observe carefully to mirror the right facial expressions.

Signal your respect and interest by nodding, agreeing, maintaining friendly eye contact, providing three to five feet of space, squaring your body with your customer, maintaining an open posture, and leaning toward your customer when appropriate. A ten percent forward lean when standing and a twenty percent forward lean when sitting creates greater rapport. Follow your customer's message with agreement cues (nodding and listening sounds) within a second or two, or your rapport will be lost.

Lead your customer to the close by gradually shifting your body language from pacing and mirroring your customer's to body language that communicates a sense of urgency and momentum. Make small incremental movements, waiting to see if your customer is following. If your customer begins to mirror and match your movement you can proceed towards the body language of closing, described in the chapter on Closing. This subtle tactic will work only if you have successfully established synchronicity with your customer through pacing, mirroring and empathy.

Some customers are much harder than others to read. Don't get discouraged. As you spend more time with your customers, you will begin to see patterns of behavior which will clarify your customer's buying style. Similarly, take the time to learn about your own style. Monitor your behaviors and especially their impact on your customer. If your intuition tells you that a style behavior does not feel right, stop and ask your customer a clarifying question. Chances are that your intuition has intercepted a mixed message from your customer.

If you can successfully master the art of reading your customer's buying style and flexing your own, you will have a competitive edge in any sales situations. There is no perfect, charismatic style that wins the customer over. Whether you are aware of it or not, whether you intend to or not, your selling style is impacting your relationship with your customers. So, the better you understand your style, the more effective you will be in flexing it.

CHAPTER 7:
PREPARING AND PRESENTING PROPOSALS TO CUSTOMERS

Nothing great was ever achieved without enthusiasm.
— *Ralph Waldo Emerson*

After gathering information concerning your customers' business and psychological needs, qualified them and made a decision to pursue the business, and have begun to build a trusting relationship with your customer, it's time to develop a specific proposal and presentation to win the business.

Developing a specific proposal means customizing or presenting your products and services so that they solve the problem or create the opportunity. Consultative sales people present the benefits of their products and services or solution, not just the features. They gain agreements from their customer that their solution solves the problem or captures the opportunity and then they ask for the order.

However, the best consultative sales people do more. They build collaborative relationships with their customer. This is more than building rapport or even building trust. It means restoring hope in your customer's mind that a solution can be found. And it means instilling confidence that working with you produces a solution that eases the pain or captures the opportunity. Without hope your customer may end the conversation, throw up objections or go through the motions of reviewing your proposal, and defer a decision.

Instilling hope and building confidence that collaborating with you will solve the problem, starts with empathy with the customer's pain. As the psychologist Carl Rodgers put it "Empathy is looking with fresh and un-frightened eyes at the customer's problem." The customer draws hope from your confidence in yourself and your company. Making well-timed and authentic empathic statements and predictions of success instill the hope on an emotional level. Showing testimonials, case studies, and research solidifies it on a rational level.

Customers sometimes accept your proposal or presentation, agree that it is a good one and do nothing. To get them to take action they must feel confident that the solution will work, that the return on investment (ROI) is worthwhile and that the risks of failure are mitigated. When writing and presenting your solution you must address ROI and risk, even if your customer has not expressed them as needs. The more specific and transparent your ROI calculations are the better. Concreteness breeds credibility. Address risk by defining the risks and offering a mitigation plan for each. A PowerPoint slide with a simple table does this effectively. Be sure to get your customer's agreement that you have identified all the risks and addressed them adequately.

Developing a Value Proposition

Good value propositions promise to quantify anticipated improvements, specify timing of benefits, specify timing of costs, estimate the payback period—the return on investment, and specify how results will be measured and tracked. For example,

> You: "Our average service response time is two hours (Feature) which means that your down time is kept to a minimum (Advantage), which means that you will not have to spend money on that back-up system you were considering (Benefit). You will save at least $5,000 per month—a savings of over $60,000 a year!" (Value)

Develop value propositions collaboratively with customers. Next, create *differentiation statements* which compare features and benefits of your solution against those of the competition. For example,

> You: "Our system is more versatile than our competitors. It allows you to make modifications on your own, without additional cost, while meeting all your requirements, including X (Differentiator). Overall, our system provides what you are looking for, at a lower initial cost and greater long-term value."

Here's another example:

> You: "According to the National Association of XYZ Providers, the average service response time is three hours. Ours is two (Differentiator). Our service quality standards have become the new benchmark in our industry. Last year we won the prestigious Service Excellence Award, and

our methodology was recently featured in a case study in the Harvard Business Review."

Your value proposition tells your customers that your solution solves their problem, while your differentiation statements suggest to your customer why your solution is better than your competitors.

Never mention competitors by name. Instead, downplay their strengths and highlight their weaknesses through *ghosting*. Ghosting is simply offering a trade-off when one of the alternatives you rejected is one of the alternatives being offered by the competition.

You: "We considered recommending the newly-released international version of the program, which is more powerful than the standard version, but rejected it as being less user-friendly than the standard version and more challenging to maintain."

Trade-offs also show your customer that you have considered alternatives and have selected the best solution for the prospect.

Making a Customer-centered Sales Pitch

To develop a 2-3 minute customer-centered sales pitch that opens up a conversation with your customer follow this five-step model.

Picture for your customer a business opportunity or challenge. This means you must research your customer's industry to uncover its current and major issues. Perhaps you are selling Internet advertising to retailers. The business opportunity might be for the retailer to increase market share of online shoppers.

Share an insight that came from your research. Uncover an unrecognized problem. Maybe it was that online shopping is increasing at a rate of 35% while your retailer customer's rate is only 10%. Support the insight with hard data. If data are not available, use testimonials, a success story, expert opinion, or media coverage of the issue. Project quantifiable results for the retailer. Improving your retailer's capture of online shoppers by just 10 more percent results in $X more in sales.

Point to the need for action. Show your customer that they must take some kind of action to capture the opportunity or solve the problem. It won't happen by itself. In our example, the retailer must reach out to the online shoppers through advertising.

Show how your solution is best. Now that you have your customer's attention you can relate your solution to the opportunity. Offer an unanticipated solution. Help customers arrive at a better solution than they would have on their own. Show your customer that your approach works better than any other. In our retailer example, you show that eyeballs on your web site belong to the same online shoppers your retailer is pursuing. The shoppers your retailer is targeting visit your website X times a week. All she has to do to reach her online shoppers is advertise on your site.

Probe for your customer's perceptions and experiences with your type of solution. Open up a conversation with your customer about the opportunity/challenge and solution. In our example, what are your retailer's thoughts about the opportunity? What pain does it cause? Has your retailer experimented with online advertising? What were the results? How did you make that decision? Who are the other stakeholders? You are now on your way to gaining agreement on the next action step, to develop a specific proposal.

Creating Proposal Themes

Your proposal should have a *theme* that in one sentence delivers the promise of your proposal. Themes are shorter, punchier and simpler than value propositions. For example, a theme might be, "Fewer production errors and happier employees with the Socrates Learning System™". While the value proposition is, "Investing in the Socrates Learning System™ and tools allows you to reduce errors by at least 15% within three months and enhance employee satisfaction as measured by your annual climate survey. All without increasing current costs."

Link a benefit to the features of your solution, stating the benefit first, since customers are usually more interested in the benefits of your solution than its features. Every opportunity worth pursuing warrants preparing a value proposition and a theme for your proposal. Take the time to get them right.

Customers Buy Benefits

Customers buy benefits, not features, so you must connect the dots for them. A *feature* answers the question, "What is it?" and "How does it work?" A *benefit* answers the question, "What can it do for me?" and "So what?" A feature is only a benefit to your customer if it answers a specific, expressed need. Until then, it's simply an *advantage*. Convert features to benefits with the phrase "…which means that..." For example, "Our response time is one hour (feature), *which means that* disruption to your work-flow is kept to a minimum (advantage) improving the productivity of your claims processors (benefit)." Another example, "Our knowledge database is searchable remotely (feature), *which means that* your people can get answers to technical questions, anywhere, anytime (advantage) which reduces those worrisome customer complaints.(benefit)."

Benefits are particularly important when responding to your customer's psychological needs. Remember that selling is a rational process that must be emotionalized. This means that you must, "Sell the sizzle, not the steak." The following are examples of responding to key psychological needs of your customer.

You:	"Our solution involves marketing, a subject you expressed interested in. (Need for growth opportunities)
You:	"A recent project we completed for a large company like yours was such a success that our customer was promoted." (Need for advancement)
You:	"Certainly, *Dr.* Gonzalez..." (Need for respect)
You:	"Our solution will raise the profile of your group within your company." (Need for recognition)
You:	"You can customize the reports and get exactly the information you need when you need it." (Need for control)
You:	"Stakeholder satisfaction will improve as emphasis shifts from recovery from problems to proactive organization improvement under our core service enhancements." (Need for job security)

Aligning with your customer's needs creates a bond between you and your customer. Respond to your customer's business needs with *functional benefits*. Functional benefits provide tangible results to your customer and fall under the broad headings of make money, save money or save time. Functional benefits address your customer's SPACED business needs discussed in Chapter 2, What Customers Want.

Developing Standard Presentations

For consultative selling you should have a standard capabilities and a standard proposal PowerPoint or video presentation. Use the *capabilities presentation* to introduce your company and your value proposition to your customers and use the *proposal presentation* to sell them a specific, tailored solution.

Closing the deal should be the sole objective of your standard proposal. The first section should include a pick list of significant customer business needs for which you have solutions. Follow that with a value proposition formula where you plug in key benefits and measurable results including the ROI you have calculated for your customer. The main section allows you to take your customer's business needs, in order of priority to your customer, and provides solutions, expressed as benefits to the customer. It also provides proof in the form of research, testimonials, white papers, case studies or industry awards. The final section should circle back to your value proposition and ask for the order. Like your capabilities presentation, your standard PowerPoint or video proposal should be an abbreviated version of your standard written proposal. A standard proposal planner like the one in Figure 8 helps you build a winning proposal while saving you time reinventing the wheel.

	Standard Proposal Planner
1.	Customer's Challenge or Opportunity and your Value Proposition
2.	Customer Business and Psychological Needs, priority ranked
3.	Your Solution to Customer Needs Need/Opportunity #1 • Your Solution • Benefits & Features • Proof • Supporting Graphics Need/Opportunity # 2 • Your Solution • Benefits & Features • Proof • Supporting Graphics Need/Opportunity # 3 • Your Solution • Benefits & Features • Proof • Supporting Graphics
	Summary • Restate value proposition • Close on Next Steps

Figure 8: Standard Proposal Planner, Adapted from Shipley Associates. *Use this proven organizer to outline all your proposals, informal or formal, written or verbal, large or small.*

PREPARING AND PRESENTING PROPOSALS...

Much of your selling process takes place virtually, through e-mail, phone, and other electronic communication. Once you have a chance to formally present, face-to-face or electronically with a customer, you had better make a good impression.

Preparing for your Presentation

Preparation of a proposal requires more time and effort than many sales organizations realize. Having some good standard presentations as templates, helps reduce the time. Assert your leadership role as the owner of the relationship building process with your senior managers, no matter how senior they might be. Preferably, you should accompany your managers to meetings with your customer.

Focusing your Presentation on your Customer

Understand the needs of your stakeholders and make sure your presentation addresses them. Group your points in easy-to-remember threes or sevens. Complex sales require extended time and multiple contacts. In a formal sales presentation you must learn beforehand who your customer-audience will include - their names, job function and hot buttons. Your customers' retention of information, your credibility, and your effectiveness depend on effective use of visuals during your sales presentation.

Rehearse your presentation at least five times. While you do not need to memorize the entire presentation word for word, you should be able to recall without notes the sequence of topics and key points.

Delivering your Presentation

Psych yourself up for your sales call or presentation by boosting your mental edge. Visualize yourself delivering a winning presentation. If you tend to get nervous before a formal presentation, remember that a little anxiety is a good thing because it supplies energy. Focus on your breathing at the beginning of your presentation and again at any time during your presentation that you feel anxious.

Introducing your Presentation

Customers are most attentive at the very beginning and the end of your presentation, so make sure you get your message across at both those points. Introduce your presentation by defining the situation and the problem/opportunity it presents for your customer, and the benefits or consequences of solving it, while establishing some rapport with your customers.

Presenting the Body of your Presentation

The body is the "meat" of your presentation and also the time when your customer's attention is most likely to wander. Remember, customers buy benefits not features so follow this up with proof of your claim. Proof may be a research report, a case study, a testimonial, an exhibit or demonstration, white papers, media coverage, or logical argument.

Beginning the Ending of your Presentation

Begin the ending by summarizing your presentation and emphasizing the benefits of your solution. At the end of a formal presentation you should expect and look forward to questions from customers.

Monitoring your Customer's Response

Customers respond to your sales presentation verbally and non-verbally ("*body language*"). When faced with a contradiction between someone's words and their body language, our intuition tells us to go with the message communicated non-verbally. If you sense that your customer is comfortable with the direction that your sales presentation is taking, you should continue as planned.

It's normal for a customer to have mixed feelings about new ideas or proposals. Your attentive reading of your customer's body language improves your understanding of their needs, clues you into their hot buttons and is a rich source of feedback for you about their receptivity to you and your ideas. The real value of observing your customer's body language is to pick up on mixed messages or changes in patterns of movements and get your customer to verbalize the issue. However you may attempt to interpret specific body language. The table below provides interpretation for some typical customer movements during a sales call.

Body Region	Customer's Body Language	Possible Meaning (in Western cultures only)
Eyes	Intent staring	"I want to control you and the agenda"
	Avoiding your eyes	"I'm uncomfortable with you" or "I'm trying to hide something from you"
	A sparkle or glint in the eye	"This is interesting!" or "I'm enjoying this relationship"
	Glassy-eyed	"I'm bored"
	Looking up and to the side	"I wonder how that might work for me?"
	Looking sideways	"Where have I heard that before?"
	Casting their eyes down	Experiencing some emotional discomfort
	Shifting eyes	Lying or looking for a way out
	Glancing towards the door	"I want this meeting to be over."
	Glancing towards an object in the room	"I want to talk about (the object)"
Hands	Drumming their fingers	Impatience - "Get to the point"
	Hands in the shape of a steeple with fingertips touching	Evaluating you, your work or your company
	Playing with a pen or pencil, shuffling papers	Concerned, annoyed, confused or wanting to say something
	Pointing at you, jabbing the desk with their finger	Angry or frustrated
	One hand tightly holding the other wrist down	On guard, threatened or very cautious
	Touching, picking up or caressing your product	Buying signal!
Face	Lightly rubbing the side of the nose with a finger when talking	Lying or at least, not sure of the veracity of what they are telling you
	Stroking the chin	Reflecting on what you are saying

Arms	Folded across the chest in a formal meeting	Protecting information or feelings
	Folded across the chest in an informal meeting	Relaxed
	One hand on the arm of the chair, the other elbow crooked and weight leaning on it	Want to get up and leave
	Hands lightly crossed or open, resting on the desk	Interested, trusting
Posture	Leaning back	Wanting to distance themselves from you
	Leaning forward	Interested
	Bolt upright, stiff	Seeking to gain control of the meeting

Figure 9: Your Customer's Body Language Means Business *Before jumping to conclusions try to verify the meaning of your customer's non-verbal communication by getting them to verbalize it.*

Your wardrobe should be appropriate for the occasion so take your cue from your sponsor and dress to his/her standard or a touch above it. Your voice is a powerful tool. Monitor and vary its speed, tone, volume and clarity. Take a deep breath before you speak so you're able to lower your pitch and to help sound authoritative. Pay attention to your body language to maximize your impact and mitigate the risk of sending mixed messages. Practice using the following gestures to emphasize your points:

Your Intent	*Use this Gesture*
Show determination	Clench your fist
Caution your customer	Point Index finger outwards, but not directly at your customer
Categorize, separate ideas	Slice the air in front of you with your hand
Compare, contrast ideas	Locate the ideas in space to your left and right
Reject an idea	Fold your arms, or push it away
Emphasize a point	Step forward, point, pause
Involve your audience	Make eye contact, open body posture

Figure 10: Use Gestures in your Presentation *Make sure that your gestures reinforce and not contradict your verbal message.*

Influencing Your Customer

The difference between influencing your customers and manipulating them is in your intent. If you have their best interests at heart, then you are influencing them. Your power to influence your customer's decisions, opinions, assumptions, and even values comes from your role or job title, your expertise, credentials or reputation, your relationship with your customer and your skills in presenting your ideas, solutions or recommendations. Customers use emotion and logic to make decisions and you must be able to influence both by providing reasons to buy and by appealing to psychological needs.

Position yourself as your customer's ally by emphasizing your independence or neutrality. Buying and selling is an emotional business whether or not your customers acknowledge it. Flex your presentation style to your customers. Refrains and slogans are effective. Be creative by finding a slogan, metaphor or refrain that represents key messages in your proposal.

Story-telling is an ancient influencing skill which leaders have used for centuries. In one experiment, some participants watched an emotionally charged movie about a father and son, and afterwards the researcher asked study participants to donate money to a stranger. Those who watched the movie were much more likely to give money to someone they'd never met than those who did not watch the emotive film.

The most successful storytellers often focus listeners' minds on a single important idea and they take no longer than a 30-second Super bowl ad spot to forge an emotional connection. Give your story a beginning, middle, and end. Tell them what the problem was like for your customer, how they felt, what happened, and what it is like now as a result of your solution. Stories are an effective way to illustrate the themes of your proposal.

Up-selling and Cross-selling

If you've been probing, listening and solving problems for your customer throughout your sales call, the next step, up-selling and cross-selling, should come naturally. Don't be reluctant about this phase of the sales cycle. There's no doubt that, "Would you like fries with that?" has worked well for McDonalds. Barriers to up-selling and cross-selling are identical to those that hinder the primary sales call. Present up-sells or cross-sells in your proposal as options that enhance your value proposition.

CHAPTER 8:
MANAGING CUSTOMER OBJECTIONS

Any fear is an illusion. You think something is standing in your way, but nothing is really there. What is there is an opportunity to do your best and gain some success. If it turns out that my best isn't good enough, then at least I'll never be able to look back and say I was too afraid to try.
—Michael Jordan

Identifying the Type of Objections

An objection is a customer's resistance to your proposal. A useful way to manage objections is to first identify the objection's type. If it's a *request for more information*, then simply provide that information in terms of benefits to your customer. Or your customer may be under a *misconception* concerning your solution. Another type of objection is the *complaint*, perhaps leftover from your customer's past experience with your company or its products. In this case, empathize, apologize, and tell the customer what your company is doing to fix the problem. A slightly tougher type of objection is *skepticism*. Your customer doubts the validity of your claims. The toughest objection of all comes from the *cynical* customer. The cynical customer does not believe your claim or your proof. Fortunately, you can win over your cynical customer by providing the opportunity for him to hear your value proposition and its proof from someone he does trust. Be prepared to offer him a name and a phone number, on the spot if possible.

Note how the sales person uses empathy, information, testimonials, and third party references to overcome misconceptions, skepticism, and cynicism in the following dialogue which picks up midway through an exploratory sales call.

Customer: "We are working on an RFP for an Executive Information System. It's a major initiative with ramifications for our entire way of operating internally, not to mention its impact on service delivery quality. I believe that the shock waves will be felt throughout the entire state, maybe even to the federal level. (Grimacing.) But I don't think you guys could handle a project of this size and scope."

You: "What makes you think that, Michael?"

Customer: "Well, your firm's core competence is strategic IT consulting – and you are excellent at it – but this is more nuts and bolts, you know, systems integration and maintenance, not quite your cup of tea."

You: "You are absolutely correct… a year ago. You probably haven't heard yet about our acquisition of Slick Systems Integrators. SSI, as you may know, is a leading player in the systems integration space. The acquisition is a real coupe for us. Would you agree that the acquisition qualifies us to bid on your project?"

Customer: "Wow. That is interesting. (Leans back, frowning, and folding his arms.) I hate to be a wet blanket, but I have seen a lot of mergers and acquisitions fail to deliver on their promises, and worse, fail their customers in the process. Now don't take this personally, but I am very reluctant to allow this company to be a guinea pig in this experiment."

You: "I don't blame you for being skeptical. Actually, other customers have felt the same. However, when they investigated the new company further, they found that the quality and reliability of service has actually improved since the acquisition." (You reach into your briefcase, take out a document on letterhead and slide it across the desk.) "Look, here's a letter from a customer, complimenting us on our performance." (Customer glances at it, but does not pick it up.)

You: "You are still not comfortable with it, are you? I can understand your reluctance. I sit in your office and tell you that we can do this project for you, I show you a letter from a customer, but those nagging doubts are

	still there, aren't they?" (Arms still crossed, Customer shrugs apologetically.)
You:	"What if I arranged for you to speak personally and privately with a customer about their experience of our services? Would that help ease your mind?"
Customer:	(Uncrosses his arms, smiles, then energetically leans across the desk, hand extended.) "You are a persistent son-of-a-gun. OK. I'll talk to your customer, and if he confirms all that you say, you'll have my blessing."

Reading the Body Language of Objections

When your customer is resistant, confused, or has an objection, you should stop talking and ask a question.

Process for Overcoming Objections

Objections can occur anywhere along the sales process, though most often they occur after your presentation.

Getting to the "Real" Objection

Listen to get to the truth of the objection. Customers can lose sight of the goal. In the heat of the sales call, a peripheral issue may sidetrack your customer. You're talking about pricing and your customer abruptly begins to grumble about past delivery problems. You find that the discussion is veering out of your control. Listen with empathy and gently guide your customer back to their objectives. Customers screen out salespeople who waste time. Perhaps your customer is indeed too busy to talk to you or is frustrated with time-wasting salespeople and has automatically assigned you to that category.

Keep in mind that your customer's feelings can interfere with their reasoning, leading them to reject risky propositions. When your customer appears to be uncertain, confused or emotional, show how your proposal mitigates the risk of losing money. Sometimes your customer does not have enough reasons to buy.

Example 1

Customer: "Not ready yet. Call me back after the budgeting cycle is over."

You: "I certainly could do that. My concern for you is that it's difficult to budget for something unless you know what you need. Let's invest some time now analyzing your needs so that you will have a better idea of what to budget later."

Example 2

Customer: "I need time to think about it."

You: "Of course. Do you mind sharing with me what specific things you need to think over? Perhaps I can set your mind at rest here and now."

Example 3

Customer: "I'm satisfied with my existing supplier."

You: "How did that relationship begin?"

"What criteria did you use to select them?"

"What do you like about them?"

"What could they improve?"

"Would you give me the same opportunity you gave your current supplier back when you gave them their first order?"

Probe for objections that you can expect your customer to raise. To isolate your customer's true objection, probe until you uncover the root of the problem.

MANAGING CUSTOMER OBJECTIONS

Here's how probing can help you control the situation:

Customer:	"I can't afford your system."
You:	"Putting cost aside for a moment, what do you like about the system I've proposed?"
Customer:	"Well, it seems like it might save me time."
You:	"And, how would you use that extra time?"
Customer:	"I might be able to reallocate staff assignments so that we could get the monthly report out without so much overtime."
You:	"What impact would that have on your overall budget?"
Customer:	"Well, for one thing, it would help me get a grip on my payroll."

And so on. Remember to hear your customer out through each response to your probes. And, let your customer know that you have heard and understood – not necessarily accepted – the objection. Confirm that the objection is real by separating a smokescreen from the true objection. It is simply a matter of probing.

Example 1

You:	"Is that [the objection] the only barrier between you and my product?"
You:	"If I can prove that our delivery schedule will meet your deadline, will you feel comfortable placing your order?"

Example 2

You:	"Let me see if I understand the situation. You are concerned about our warranty, (restating the objection) is that right?"

Customer: "Yes."

You: "What concerns you about that?"

Customer: "It's too short."

You: "So if it weren't for the length of our warranty you would be a customer right now. Is that right?" (If they say "Yes," then you have identified the final objection. Then answer it and close the sale.)

Match benefits to your customer's real need and fit your solution to your customer's objection. Try the *"feel, felt, found"* technique. For example,

You: "I know how you *feel* and I don't blame you for being skeptical. Actually, other customers have *felt* the same. However, when they investigated the new company further, they *found* that the quality and reliability of service has actually improved since the acquisition."

When blind-sided by an objection, flip the tables by using the *reverse* technique:

Customer: "I don't think there's much point in taking this any further. We are happy with our current supplier."

You: "That's exactly why I'm here, Mr. Customer, to give you the opportunity to evaluate your supplier's competition to confirm that you are getting the best value for your money."

Always ask for the order after you have overcome an objection.

Overcoming the Price Objection

Customers like to buy rationally, analytically, based on the numbers, transaction by transaction, impersonally, with risk built into the price, and with deep product knowledge. However, more often than not, they buy psychologically, based on relationships, without full product knowledge, and with an aversion to risk. Refer to the price in a positive light, i.e. "an investment." Distinguish between price and cost. *Price* is

MANAGING CUSTOMER OBJECTIONS

the amount stated on the price tag. *Cost* is price minus savings over the lifespan of the product.

Attack the price objection with probing questions such as:

You: "Too high compared to what, Mr. Customer?"

You: "Does that mean that I have failed to demonstrate the value of my proposal or is it that you do not have the budget?"

You: "Do you have a target price in mind - a cost per user, or a fixed price, a licensing agreement?"

You: "Are you comparing our CD/training program/whatever to another program you have purchased... to another, competing proposal?" (If "yes," then ask them to lay it out on the table, to see if it is "apples to apples".)

Sometimes price is a smokescreen for some other issue.

You: "Before we talk more about price, are there any other concerns you may have about our proposal?"

You: "If I could show you how easy it is to cost-justify our program, would you go ahead today?"

You: "Besides price, is there anything else standing in the way of us doing business?"

At other times the price objection is not an objection at all, but a buying signal. They have made up their mind to buy, and now want to negotiate. In that case, close the sale.

You: "Are you ready to move on now and talk money?"

Customer: "Yes."

You: "So I'm safe in assuming that you agree that our proposal solves your problem and that we are capable of executing the agreement?"

Customer: "Yes"

You: "And that our price represents great value?"

Customer: "Good, not great value."

You: "Do you have an order number I should put on my invoice?"

If your customer says "No," explain the value in your pricing. Give them a justification for your price, confirm that they agree and then ask for the order again.

CHAPTER 9:
GETTING AGREEMENTS
WITH CUSTOMERS

Nothing happens in business until someone sells something.

To get agreements from your customer and take some specific action towards the sale, you must build a sense of urgency and momentum. Drive your presentation to a commitment to next steps by responding immediately to buying signals. *Buying signals* are your customers' non-verbal indications that they are ready to make a decision. They can occur anytime in the sales process.

Closing on Buying Signals

In general, when a customer is considering your proposal, weighing up the pros and cons, psychological energy is expended. When the customer has made the decision -- either for or against your proposal – the tension disappears and the customer relaxes. If you are paying attention, you will see customers release a slight sigh of relief that the decision-making is over. Shoulders may slump, and the body may relax into the chair. When customers really are interested in your product or service, they may touch or stroke the product, pick it up and hold it, glance at it frequently, relax and smile, ask a flurry of questions, ask for details of installation or delivery, ask about payment terms or warranties, shift from saying "you" to "us" and restate product benefits, or elaborate on how it will solve a problem.

These behaviors may be unconscious signals that the customer is ready to be closed. You should stop what you are doing and ask for the order. The old salesperson's maxim, "The ABCs of selling – Always Be Closing" is good advice, because you must be receptive to the customer's buying signals and know how to respond appropriately.

Using Closing Techniques

The *Trial Close*, helps you to gain agreement from your customer on an issue that must be resolved before the actual sale.

    You: "On a scale of one to 10, how much do you like the idea?"

    Customer: "Eight."

    You: "What do we have to do to get a 10?"

The *Summary Close* is best when you've uncovered a number of your customer's needs and proposed a specific solution. It's the close you'll use most often in consultative selling. For example:

    You: "Your goal is to reduce overhead by 20 percent next year. You're trying to do that by centralizing your copying services and updating your technology. You have agreed that our proposal does that and more. Let's get the paper work wrapped up and you can start realizing those savings."

The *Alternative Close* invites your customer to choose from two or more positive outcomes. You eliminate a negative choice while allowing your customer to feel in control. For example:

    You: "Have you decided on monthly or quarterly billing?"

It's often appropriate to assume that your customer has already made the buying decision and you already have the order. Help your customer get over the difficult hurdle of making the buying decision. The *Assumptive Close* just wraps up the details. You might say, "I'll send that contract over by courier today for your signature." Use this close with every customer. Be very careful of assuming too much or your customer may perceive your close as manipulative or pushy. Remember you earn the right to ask for the order by working hard throughout the sales process. Your customer must be on the brink of a decision for the alternative or assumptive closes to work. For example:

    You: "If you were to go ahead with the service, what would be the first thing you would do after installation? OK,

GETTING AGREEMENTS WITH CUSTOMERS

	I'll make a note of that and pass it onto our Customer Care people."
You:	"If you were to go ahead with the order, what day of the week would be best for delivery? So, I'll schedule your first shipment for 11 AM." (On the day of the week they give you.)
You:	"Will you pay the first installment by check or purchasing card?"

If your customer agrees to your close, show that you're pleased and appreciate your customer's business. When the customer signals the end of the call, shake hands, say goodbye and leave. If, despite your best efforts, your customer backs out, don't let yourself sound discouraged or frustrated. "No" doesn't necessarily mean "never." Sell your customer on future opportunities. Whatever close you use, remember to use silence as a lever. Ask for the order, and then wait silently for your customer's response – no more selling.

The Physical Action Close, as the name implies, invites your customer to make a commitment by initialing, checking off or signing your proposal, or pieces of it. For example,

You:	"Ms. Customer, here is my understanding of your department's information needs. First, you need an in-house, comprehensive and up to date reference library of political and economic information. This would ensure that no longer would anyone make a decision based on inadequate information. And it will spare you the embarrassment of a repeat of the situation involving the CEO you described to me earlier. (Customer nods approvingly. You slide a paper and expensive looking pen across the desk to your customer.) OK, would you just put a check mark beside that one for me please?"
Customer:	"OK." (She checks it.)
You:	"The second area that needs attention concerns access to information. You felt that all senior executives should have online access to the information. We also recommend that you provide access for all research

	professionals as well. Our survey indicated that speed and ease of access to information would increase their productivity significantly. Does that make sense?"
Customer:	"Well, of course they would say that, but then on the other hand I appreciate how frequently they need to access the information. Yes, we should definitely consider including them."
You:	(Pointing to the item on the paper, looking expectantly at your customer who picks up the pen and places a check against it,) "Thank you".

If you have removed all remaining questions from the customer's mind and you have proven the value of your proposition, you have earned the right to ask for the order. Watch for buying signals and close the sale.

CHAPTER 10:
NEGOTIATING WITH CUSTOMERS

Never give, always trade.

The old saying, "everything is negotiable," is true in business and in your social and personal life as well. Every day you negotiate with friends and family to sort out who is doing what and when, to arrange a time to pick someone up, to go shopping, or to settle who gets the last of the ice-cream. Children are natural negotiators, except that they often favor manipulation and bullying. At work you may negotiate prices and timetables with customers, quotas with your manager, and assistance from support staff. Perhaps you revert to the childhood tactics because you have never learned alternatives. You either push too hard to get the order or give in to your customer's demands too readily. With just a few skills and techniques, and a little knowledge of the principles of negotiation, you can close more deals, help your customers get what they want, and feel good about the process.

Recognizing When Your Customer is Negotiating

When customers are hard-nosed about getting a lower price, 80 percent of the time it is because they do not appreciate the value of your product and have not made a commitment to buy. Step back and re-sell the benefits.

Customer: "You've got to do better than that on price."

You: "I'm glad you mentioned price, Ms. Customer, let's take another look at how our solution is going to save you money/make you money/increase productivity."

Seek a clear agreement from your customer that your solution works before negotiating the price. Make sure that your customer is empowered to do business with you.

Customer:	"OK, let's talk price."
You:	"Sure. Just so that I'm clear before we move on: We are in agreement that our solution, with the modifications we discussed, is exactly what you are looking for, right?"
Customer:	"Well I don't know about that. I've got to run this by my boss."

Never assume that your customer remembers or even understands how much money your solution saves them, or what return they can expect on their investment.

Customer:	"I need at least a 20 percent discount."
You:	"Why 20 percent, why not 19?"
Customer:	"Because there is no way that this is worth the price you are estimating."
You:	"That depends on what return you expect on this investment. What do you usually consider as good return – three times, 10 times? Earlier, we estimated that you could get an additional 10% more business from your customers with our solution. I calculated that translates into an additional $5 million, and that's just on your major accounts. Not a bad return on a $100,000 investment don't you think?"

Preparing to Negotiate

Don't underestimate your power in a negotiation. Your relationship with your customer, your understanding of how your proposed solution meets your customer's needs, and your knowledge of the negotiating process itself forms the basis of your power. The more knowledge you have, the broader your power base. For example, you may know the limits of your ability to discount price. But do you also know how much room you have to maneuver with delivery schedules, product quantity or quality, and payment terms? If you don't, you may lose the deal, or win the deal but lose your profit margin. You and your customers may decide to negotiate price, but you may forget to negotiate terms, conditions, delivery schedules, resources, ownership, work location, time and scope.

You may have a variety of objectives in a negotiation. Sometimes you may want to "buy" your way into your customer account by delivering at cost, because this one is a cornerstone customer. Other times, you may want to demonstrate to your buyer that the days of "off the rate card pricing" are over. Or, because there is a large backlog of orders, you must hold the line on delivery times but give a little on payment terms.

Always get what you want from a sale by being prepared to negotiate. Don't be taken by surprise when your customer ends the meeting just as you are about to ask for the order, or when they want to revisit the price after a handshake agreement. You will always be prepared to negotiate successfully if you have thought about what would be your best outcome, beforehand, the most likely outcome and the worst outcome. Knowing your bottom line also enhances your confidence in negotiating. This is the most critical part of preparation. If you don't know your best outcome, don't expect to get it. Conversely, if you are not clear about your minimal acceptable outcome, you may regret it. Also determine your customer's best case, most likely case, and least acceptable case.

Prevent your feelings from interfering with your effectiveness by calculating your bottom line before you get into an emotionally charged negotiation. Consider this scenario, reported by The New Yorker magazine. You are sitting on a park bench with a stranger. A Consultant comes up and offers both of you $10. The stranger gets to decide how the money should be divided. You get to veto the division, but if you do, neither of you gets anything. Good sense says take any division even a dollar. But most people reject offers of less than three dollars. Reason? Their pride interferes with their good sense.

Customers often make initial flat demands. They may say, "We've got to have Phase One finished by Thursday." A little probing might reveal the drivers of that position and uncover the real need. Maybe your customer wants to report completion of Phase One at a regular meeting with his boss. Or perhaps your customer is under the mistaken belief that it takes you two days to turnaround a report on Phase One, or perhaps he is expecting push back from you and wants to give himself some cushion. A critical skill throughout the sales process, probing is especially crucial o get past this first round negotiating gambit.

Consider this example. Two little girls come home from school, running into the kitchen and heading straight to the refrigerator. They begin to fight over who gets the one and only orange. Mother intervenes, and what does she do? Cuts it in half, of course, and gives the girls half each. One little girl hungrily devours her half, tossing the rind in the garbage. The other girl fishes out the rind from the garbage, peels her half and throws out the fruit. Armed with the rind of the orange she proceeds to use it for a craft project for homework.

In this scenario, the girls' initial demands were that they had to have the orange and had it not been for Mom's intervention they may have gone to war over it. Mom did what you may well have done yourself to settle the negotiation-- She took the easy way out and forced a compromise. Had she done a little probing, she would have learned that the girls' real needs were not the same. One wanted the fruit and the other wanted the rind. The girls allowed their feelings to interfere with their effectiveness. They perceived the situation as a threat and they became afraid that they might not get what they wanted. That fear impaired their judgment concerning how to resolve the issue and drove them into a confrontation.

An instinctive response to negotiating is to protect your ground and aim to win the negotiation, as though there can only be a winner and a loser. In fact, several outcomes are possible along two different lines. There will be an outcome for the *substance* of the deal itself, (i.e. the terms, conditions, price etc.) and there will be an outcome concerning your *relationship* with your customer. Most of the time the substance of the deal will be as important to you as strengthening your customer relationship. You will want repeat business from your customer. There will be times when the substance of the deal is very important to you, but you don't expect to, or don't want do business with this customer again. Perhaps you can make a bundle of money on a deal but your customer's business practices are so distasteful to you that you decide that this is the only deal you will do with them.

A *win-win* outcome occurs when you and your customer both get what you want. Win-win is your goal when negotiating with a customer who you want to do business with repeatedly, and where the substance of the deal is important to you. Often win-win outcomes require that you use empathy and probing skills to find a creative solution to the problem of different and mutually exclusive wants.

A *win-lose* outcome occurs when you get what you want but your customer is less than satisfied. Win-lose is your best approach when you do not trust your customer to play by the rules. You don't expect to do business with them again and the substance of the deal is very important to you.

Lose-win is when your customer gets the better of you, an outcome that is rarely desirable except in those instances where your relationship with your customer is very important to you but the substance of the deal is not.

Finally, a *Lose/Lose* outcome occurs when neither of you gets all of what you want. You compromise so that you both get some, but not all of what you want. Typically, compromise is used to resolve a difference in price by splitting the difference. In this respect, compromise is a lose/lose outcome. You and your customer may agree to compromise for the sake of harmony, convenience, to avoid uncomfortable conflict or because neither the substance nor the relationship is important. For example, at a garage sale you might compromise because you don't really need that table and you probably won't see the seller again. You might brag about getting a good deal but in fact you haven't because you had to compromise. Compromising is the easy way out, and not the hallmark of a truly authentic sales person, whereas *creative problem-solving* is challenging and is the way to a win-win outcome. To minimize the temptation to compromise, state your intentions clearly upfront.

You: "Ms. Customer, my intention is to negotiate a solution that works for you and works for me as well. At this early stage I do not have such a solution. However, I am confident that if we are both committed to a win/win outcome, if we are fair and reasonable, if we talk more about what we want and explore some creative avenues, then that win/win will present itself."

This kind of statement has the added benefit of reducing any defensiveness your customer may have towards the negotiation. Assume good faith, fair play and expect fairness. Assume that your customers are trustworthy, operate with good intentions and are honest until proven otherwise. Customers may be guarded and they may even be defensive, but they may still want to operate in good faith. A little listening, probing and empathizing, while agreeing to nothing, can help determine good faith.

Trust improves negotiation outcomes. Take the time to build a relationship with your customer before negotiating. If your customers get to know you, they are more likely to trust you. And if they trust you, you are more likely to get win-win outcomes. If you want proof, *Oxytocin* is a hormone that the brain produces during breast-feeding, sex and intimate cuddling and other types of social bonding. Oxytocin appears also to make people more trusting. For example, give some money to another person to invest on your behalf and then allow them to decide how much to return to you and how much to keep. Those given Oxytocin will return to you significantly more of the profit than a control group.

Trading, not giving

Now you are ready to move into the fun part of negotiating – trading. Start high and make your first proposal sound like your last. If your customer does not accept it, express your disappointment. An effective way to convey this is to flinch and cast your eyes down for a moment. Then re-commit to a win/win outcome. Take one issue at a time, starting with the easiest. Starting with the easiest issue allows you and your customer to achieve an early success, and to have some common agreements to build on.

Float a tentative solution, using the formula, "If you will, then I will." Never give, always trade. This trial solution should include a concession from you, at a cost of a concession from your customer. At this point, your concession should not be a major one; it should be somewhere between your best-case outcome and your most likely case outcome.

Slow down your breathing, use deliberate gestures and facial expressions, keep your head up and look your customer directly in the eyes. This helps you maintain control of the negotiating process. If your customer counter-offers, once again flinch and allow some disappointed silence to fall. Continue this process until your customer agrees.

Move on to the next issue, remembering to save the toughest issue to last. Never indicate impatience. You want your customer to believe that if necessary to gain agreement, you can do this all day. Keep in mind that feelings prefer immediate gratification to long term gain, even when the long term gain is greater. If you are anxious during a negotiation, you may make concessions to relieve the anxiety. If you are calm, you are more likely to take the long view and trade rather than concede.

Throughout the process, confirm and record agreements, no matter how small. You should also show appreciation whenever your customer adheres to the ground rules. When all the issues have been settled, summarize and record the outcomes. Follow up with written confirmation of your agreements with your customer, again complimenting them on their respect for the ground rules.

Sometimes your customer may want to ratify your negotiated outcome, usually by having their boss sign off on the agreement. If this is the case, note in writing, "subject to ratification." This also implies that you can re-open negotiation of any of the issues if sign-off becomes a problem.

Countering Customer Negotiation Tactics

Be prepared for customer negotiating tactics by determining your response before your sales call. Don't be blindsided into giving away something you did not intend to. Your customers may attempt to improve their outcome at your expense (lose-win). *Negotiating tactics* tend to turn the focus away from legitimate, negotiable items and ask for concessions based on irrelevant issues. Sometimes negotiation tactics are used unconsciously (see examples below). Tactics have persisted and are touted in some negotiation books and training workshops because they are effective, at least in the short-term. Their long-term effect is to hinder relationship building because your customer does not want to feel that you are taking unfair advantage.

It is amazing how many concessions you make when flattered. It feels so good to be praised that you want to thank the person, and what better way than to give them what they want. Resist it politely and stay firm.

Customer:	"Would you do me favor? Just add this survey question? I'd do it myself except that you are so much better at it than I am."
You:	"Thanks for that. Normally I'd be happy to do it, but unfortunately it's too late. The survey has gone to printing."

Watch out for the *"Poor innocent me"* ploy, sometimes used unconsciously. Empathy when teamed with firm resistance, again wins the day.

Customer:	"This has been the week from hell. I've had extra projects dumped on me, my wife is having surgery Monday, and my car is in the shop as a result of an accident. Could you do me a big favor and not charge me for X?"
You:	"Believe me, I know exactly how you feel. I've had days like that too. I wish I could help but we have already agreed on a price for X."

You have come to an agreement, have it documented, perhaps even ratified, and all that is left to do is get signatures. With pen poised to sign, your customer pauses, points to an item, usually the price, and says "How about knocking another 5% off and I'll sign this immediately?" From where he sits, what does he have to lose by *escalating demands*? In your haste to close, you just might cave in. The correct response here is simply "no."

If you want to disagree with your customers, mention your reasons first (or they may not get listened to.) If they are accepted, you may not have to point out that you disagree. To make your point, use benchmarks such as standard operating procedures or professional standards rather than opinion or speculation. Don't rebut every point your customer makes, even if you are convinced your customer is wrong. If you feel that you must launch an attack on your customer, do it abruptly, rather than building up to it in a way that allows them time to develop a counter attack.

Customers may try to get a lower price by asking for a breakdown of your system's components and then trying to negotiate a lower price, component by component, or by putting out to bid individual components. Similar to the escalating demands tactic, at the last minute, the customer tries to return to an item agreed to earlier and tries to open it up again for negotiation. The hope is that by creating confusion, they will be able to get a better deal on the current item.

> Customer: "You guys are tough. This is still more than I would like to pay. What is the breakdown and how much do you pay for labor? How much for overhead? What if I bought…?"

> You: "Mr. Customer, I'm confused. Earlier you agreed on the total budget and that it represented outstanding value. By your own calculations, you expect a 10:1 return. And that's what really important here, isn't it? Not my costs. So, what day is best for your kick-off meeting, Thursday or Friday?"

Escalating authority is a classic tactic that attempts to get you to make concessions, especially on price, by claiming that your proposal has to go to a higher level because it is 10% or five percent higher than the "company guidelines." The hope here is that you will be reluctant to, in effect, start all over again with someone else and will make the concession. The "company guideline" might well be fictional.

"What if I bought..." is a tactic similar to the escalating demands tactic. At the last minute, your customer tries to return to an item agreed to earlier and tries to open it up again for negotiation. The hope is that by creating confusion, she will be able to get a better deal on the current item.

You:	"Ms. Customer, sorry, but I'm confused. We agreed to that item yesterday, and in fact, at the time you seemed to be pretty pleased with the solution. Has something changed? If not, let's move on. We're on a roll here."

Walk away and wait is another effective tactic when your customer senses you would like to close as soon as possible. Your customer abruptly brings the meeting to an end, without responding to your proposal. Your phone calls are not returned, no email, sometimes for weeks. The hope is that you will assume that your price is too high, and when you eventually re-establish contact, that you will have already lowered it. Be patient. Stay in touch, continuing to show your interest but not your anxiety, in resolving the issue or closing the deal. Conversely, don't immediately make a counter proposal when your customer makes an offer. Remember everything is negotiable, including arbitrary deadlines for a response.

CHAPTER 11:
SUMMARY AND NEXT STEPS

Now that you have read this book, take some time to reflect on what you have learned that will improve your selling. In any case, the next step is up to you. You are responsible for your own professional development. Start by tackling the improvement that will yield the best return on your investment of time and effort. Now consider what you must do to keep the momentum going in your professional development. In the meantime you must practice the skills you wish to acquire so that they become automatic and fully integrated into your selling style. Whatever you do, monitor your energy and enthusiasm for sales. There is no limit on the amount of financial success you can have in sales and no end to the amount of satisfaction you can get by getting there through consultative selling.

Free Initial Sales Consultation with the Author

To find a convenient time for a 30-minute free initial consultation with Dr. John Brennan, please copy this URL into your web browser:

https://www.timetrade.com/book/GGLSM

Or call 1-585-230-5765.

Made in the USA
Columbia, SC
20 June 2017